# ENIGMAS *of* HISTORY

# SEARCHING FOR ATLANTIS

WORLD BOOK

a Scott Fetzer company
Chicago
www.worldbook.com

World Book edition of "Enigmas de la historia" by Editorial Sol 90.

Enigmas de la historia
Atlántida, la leyenda del continente perdido

This edition licensed from Editorial Sol 90 S.L.
Copyright 2013 Editorial Sol S.L. All rights reserved.

English-language revised edition copyright 2014, 2016
World Book, Inc.
Enigmas of History
Searching for Atlantis

World Book, Inc.
180 North LaSalle Street
Suite 900
Chicago, Illinois 60601
USA

For information about other World Book publications, visit
our website at **www.worldbook.com** or call **1-800-967-5325.**

**Library of Congress Cataloging-in-Publication Data**

Atlantida, la leyenda del continente perdido. English.
  Searching for Atlantis. -- English-language revised edition.
    p. cm. --  (Enigmas of history)
  Includes bibliographical references and index.
  Summary: "An exploration of the legend of the lost island
of Atlantis. Features include maps, reconstructions of Atlan-
tis, links to other cultures, places to see and visit, a glossary,
and index"-- Provided by publisher.
    ISBN 978-0-7166-2662-6
    1. Atlantis (Legendary place)--Juvenile literature. I. World
Book, Inc. II. Title.
GN751.A7713 2014
001.94--dc23
                                        2014010109

Set ISBN: 978-0-7166-2660-2

Printed in China by PrintWORKS Global Services
Shenzhen, Guangdong
2nd printing July 2016

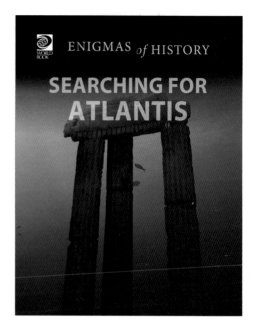

An artist's conception of the island Atlantis that, in
legend, is said to have sunk beneath the Atlantic
Ocean. First mentioned by the Greek **philosopher**
Plato in the 300's B.C., Atlantis has fascinated people
since that time and engendered countless theories
and stories.

© Zac Macaulay, Getty Images

# Staff

## Executive Committee

President
  Jim O'Rourke

Vice President and Editor in Chief
  Paul A. Kobasa

Vice President, Finance
  Donald D. Keller

Vice President, Marketing
  Jean Lin

Director, Human Resources
  Bev Ecker

## Editorial

Managing Editor,
  Annuals and Topical Reference
  Christine Sullivan

Editors
  Jake Bumgardner
  Lynn Durbin
  Nicholas Kilzer

Manager, Indexing Services
  David Pofelski

Administrative Assistant
  Ethel Matthews

Manager, Contracts & Compliance
  (Rights & Permissions)
  Loranne K. Shields

Senior Manager, Publishing
  Operations
  Timothy Falk

## Manufacturing/Production

Manufacturing Manager
  Sandra Johnson

Production/Technology
  Manager
  Anne Fritzinger

Proofreader
  Nathalie Strassheim

## Graphics and Design

Senior Art Director
  Tom Evans

Senior Designer
  Don Di Sante

Media Researcher
  Rosalia Bledsoe

Manager, Cartographic Services
  Wayne K. Pichler

Senior Cartographer
  John M. Rejba

**Glossary** There is a glossary of terms on
page 44. Terms defined in the glossary are in
boldface (type that looks like this) on their first
appearance on any *spread* (two facing pages).
Words that are difficult to say are followed by a
pronunciation (pruh NUHN see AY shuhn) the
first time they are mentioned.

# Contents

# A Continent Submerged in Time

The story of Atlantis is one of the greatest legends of all time. Perhaps it has survived for some 3,600 years because of its many mysteries. Did the continent ever really exist? If it did, where was it? Was it actually destroyed by a *cataclysm* (such events as great floods or earthquakes)? Perhaps the legend has been told and retold because the sudden, terrible fate of the Atlanteans is endlessly fascinating. Perhaps the story fascinates because the destruction of a civilization by a horrible natural disaster seems so believable.

The story of a lost island called Atlantis first appeared in the 300's B.C. in works by the Greek **philosopher** Plato. He described Atlantis as the home of a brilliant civilization. But the people became corrupt, and so the gods decided to punish them. Atlantis was wracked by earthquakes and floods, and within one day and night, the island sank into the sea.

Many people have searched for the remains of this lost island. People have guessed it was once located in the Mediterranean Sea, the Atlantic Ocean, and the Caribbean Sea, among other places. Today, many scholars link Atlantis to Santorini, an island group in the Aegean Sea, north of the Greek island of Crete. Volcanic eruptions and the huge waves they created destroyed most of Santorini in about 1600 B.C. The dis-aster also may have devastated Crete, the center of the glorious **Minoan** civilization. Such upheaval would have shocked the Mediterranean world. Tales of the disaster, passed down over generations, may have inspired Plato to create his story of a fallen people and their vengeful gods.

# The Legend of Atlantis

Atlantis was wealthy, beautiful, and technologically advanced. But then its people turned away from **virtue** and peace.

The story of Atlantis, as told by Plato, is actually a tale about how a small, virtuous city defeated a city mired in decay and immorality. The virtuous city was Athens, Plato's birthplace. The immoral city was Atlantis.

According to Plato, the battle between Athens and Atlantis took place some 9,000 years before he wrote the story. Plato said the story of Atlantis had been passed down through his family from Solon, the great Athenian lawgiver, who was an ancestor of his mother.

Plato wrote that Solon had heard the story from priests of ancient Egypt while on a visit there in about 600 B.C., generations earlier. According to Plato, Solon told the priests

a Greek story about how Zeus, the lord of the gods, sent a flood to destroy people because he was displeased with their behavior. The priests laughed at Solon, telling him that there had been many floods and that one of them had destroyed one of the greatest civilizations of history.

## FOUNDING ATLANTIS

As Plato tells it, after the gods created the world, they met to decide who would rule over its various parts. Athena, the goddess of wisdom, received Greece. Poseidon, the god of the sea and earthquakes, was given the island of Atlantis. This vast island lay just beyond the **Pillars of Hercules** (the Strait of Gibraltar), huge rocks that marked the border between the Mediterranean Sea and the Atlantic Ocean.

In their areas, the gods made temples to themselves and taught the people how to offer **sacrifices** to them.

At that time, there lived on Atlantis a beautiful girl named Cleito. Poseidon fell in love with her and went to live with her on a mountain in the center of the island. Over time, Poseidon and Cleito had five sets of twin sons.

One of the sons, named Atlas, became the island's first king, giving Atlantis and the surrounding ocean his name. He ruled over the center of the island. The rest of the island was divided among his brothers.

## WISE KINGS

According to Plato, the kings were guided by a code of conduct inspired by Poseidon. Every five or six years, the rulers held a council. There,

they discussed their common policies and swore to abide by their laws. One of these laws stated that the kings could never fight among themselves. Another forbade a ruler from taking the life of one of his people without the consent of at least a majority of the other rulers.

The dialogue among the kings was the foundation of good government for the Atlanteans. Plato also wrote that the peace enjoyed by the kingdoms was the Atlanteans' reward for working together.

### HONORING POSEIDON

At the council, the kings held a ceremony dedicated to Poseidon. The ceremony began with the kings hunting a bull, without wearing armor or using iron weapons. Once captured, the bull was slaughtered at the foot of a large pillar. Written on the pillar were the **sacred** laws of Atlantis and the terrible punishments for those who violated them.

After the blood of the bull was collected in a container, the bull was burned. The kings sprinkled themselves with the blood to purify themselves and threw some into the fire. The kings then promised that they and all their descendants would keep the sacred laws.

Once the ritual was completed, the kings drank the bull's blood, left their cups in the temple of Poseidon, and prepared for new deliberations.

Dressed in blue tunics, the kings sat among the

**GREEK BRAVERY**
Only the great valor and military skill of Athenian soldiers prevented the Atlanteans from conquering the known world, Plato wrote.

**MARKETPLACE**
A bustling marketplace called the *agora* was the center of activity in ancient Greek cities.

ashes of the **sacrificed** bull. They then judged each other and any people accused of committing crimes. The kings also handed out punishments. Each sentence was recorded on a golden tablet, which was kept together with the blue tunics worn for the occasion.

**GOVERNING ATLANTIS**
Each king had many officials to help him rule over his land. These officials looked out for the well being of their community, protected the lands and fields, developed business activities, and organized the storage of goods.

Atlantis's military officials were particularly important. They were responsible for maintaining a large force of warriors and ships. They made sure these

forces were ready at all times to defend the island and the surrounding sea from enemy attack. The military officials also saw that their warriors had enough war chariots and weapons.

**ATLANTIS THRIVES**
The kings of Atlantis were considered direct descendants of Poseidon. As a result, their subjects faithfully followed their judgments. According to Plato, the rulers' **virtue** was boundless as long as they remained under the direct influence of the gods.

For many generations, Atlantis's kings ruled with gentleness and wisdom. Because of its virtuous rulers and people, Atlantis became a "great and wonderful empire." This empire included lands in Europe and Africa, both inside and outside the **Pillars of Hercules.**

**THE ATTACK ON ATHENS**
Over time, however, the influence of the gods became less important to Atlanteans than earthly pleasures. They became corrupt, prizing treasure over virtue. Atlantis's kings turned to war as a means of satisfying their appetite for power and material wealth. They abandoned their commitment to peace and set out to conquer all the lands inside the Pillars, including the countries of the ancient Greek-speaking people known as the **Hellenes.**

This is when Athens "shone forth" to lead the

fight against the Atlanteans. Among all the countries under attack, Plato wrote, the Athenians had the greatest courage and military skill.

As the war raged on, Athens's allies fell away. One by one, they surrendered or were defeated, until only Athens stood against Atlantis. Then, at the very edge of disaster, Athens triumphed against its enemy.

The Greeks' victory preserved the freedom of the Hellenes. Moreover, said Plato, the Athenians generously freed all the other people living within the Pillars of Hercules who had been enslaved by the Atlanteans.

**THE DESTRUCTION OF ATLANTIS**
The defeated Atlanteans returned home, only to face an even greater disaster. Zeus had become increasingly angry with them for abandoning the laws of the gods and for their aggressive acts. He gathered all the gods together and demanded that the Atlanteans be punished.

Soon, devastating earthquakes began to rock the island. Sparks from cooking fires and lamps triggered raging fires. Mountainous waves swept far inland, covering the houses and fields. In a single day and night, Plato said, all of Atlantis's "warlike men" sank into the earth, and, with their disappearance, the island of Atlantis was swallowed by the sea.

# The Man Behind the Legend

The ancient Greek **philosopher** Plato was the first to write about Atlantis.

P lato wrote the story of Atlantis to show how an ideal society could be created by following the right path of good government, mutual respect, and neighborly kindness. The people of Atlantis gained wealth and greatness because they had a harmonious relationship with the gods, nature, and one another.

Plato then turned his tale into a warning about the terrible consequences of violating the basic principles that led to the island's success. When the kings and people became greedy and power hungry, the great island was destroyed.

Most scholars agree that Atlantis was not an actual civilization. Some scholars think Plato meant "Atlantis" in its golden era to represent Athens at a distant time when its government and people were more **virtuous.**

Nevertheless, Plato was careful to make Atlantis seem like an actual place. His description of the island and its people is detailed and realistic.

Plato also tried to make his story more believable by claiming that Solon, a famous politician, lawmaker, and highly respected historical figure, brought the story to Greece.

## POLITICAL AMBITION

Like Solon, Plato was interested in politics. In 404 B.C., Plato was offered a chance to enter politics by his cousin Critias. Critias was the leader of a group of wealthy *tyrants* (dictators) elected to replace the democratic government of Athens after a devastating war and **plague.**

However, Plato refused the offer because of the group's cruel and unethical practices, including bringing in Spartan soldiers to crush opposition to the rule of the tyrants. The group lasted only one year before the Athenians *deposed* them (turned them out of office).

Plato considered entering Athens's new democratic government. But he decided not to seek office after his friend, the **philosopher** Socrates, was brought to trial and sentenced to death in 399 B.C. Socrates had been accused of casting doubt on widely accepted religious and political beliefs. Plato left Athens and traveled for a number of years.

In 387 B.C., Plato returned to Athens and founded a school of *philosophy* (a type of study concerned with such ideas as existence and reality) and science that became known as the Academy. The Academy was one of the first centers for higher education. Plato lived in Athens and headed the Academy for the rest of his life. His most distinguished pupil at the Academy was the Greek philosopher Aristotle.

**THE ACADEMY**
Plato (left, in painting) and his student Aristotle appear in the center in a detail of the *School of Athens* (1510-1511), a painting by the great Italian artist Raphael.

# Plato's Dialogues

Plato wrote in a literary form called the **dialogue,** which is a conversation between two or more people. Plato's dialogues are actually dramas that are concerned chiefly with the presentation, criticism, and conflict of philosophical ideas. Many of Plato's dialogues try to identify the nature or essence of some philosophically important notion by defining it. The central question of the dialogue *The Republic* is, "What is justice?" The story of Atlantis appears in two of Plato's dialogues—*Critias* and *Timaeus.* These dialogues, each named for people in them, explore **virtue.**

# Solon (639?-559? B.C.)

Solon was a famous lawmaker of Athens who was known as one of the seven wise men of Greece. In 594 B.C., the Athenians gave Solon the authority to change the city's laws. He enacted many political and economic reforms. For example, he ended the practice of enslaving people who could not pay back money they owed. He divided citizens into classes by wealth and defined the rights and duties of each class. He changed the money system to make foreign trade easier.

Solon is said to have made the Athenians promise to keep his laws for 10 years. He then left Athens. But when he returned 10 years later, he found the city fighting a civil war. After opposing the eventual victor in that conflict, Solon retired from public life.

# Plato's Atlantis

The Greek **philosopher** wrote of an island city with a circular layout inhabited 9,000 years ago. Its rise and fall became a **myth** that continues to inspire scientific explorations in the seas and oceans of the world.

## The City of Canals

Atlantis consisted of two rings of land separated by waterways. The central island was dominated by the **Citadel,** which held temples and a grove dedicated to Poseidon, the royal palace, government buildings, and the mansions of the wealthy.

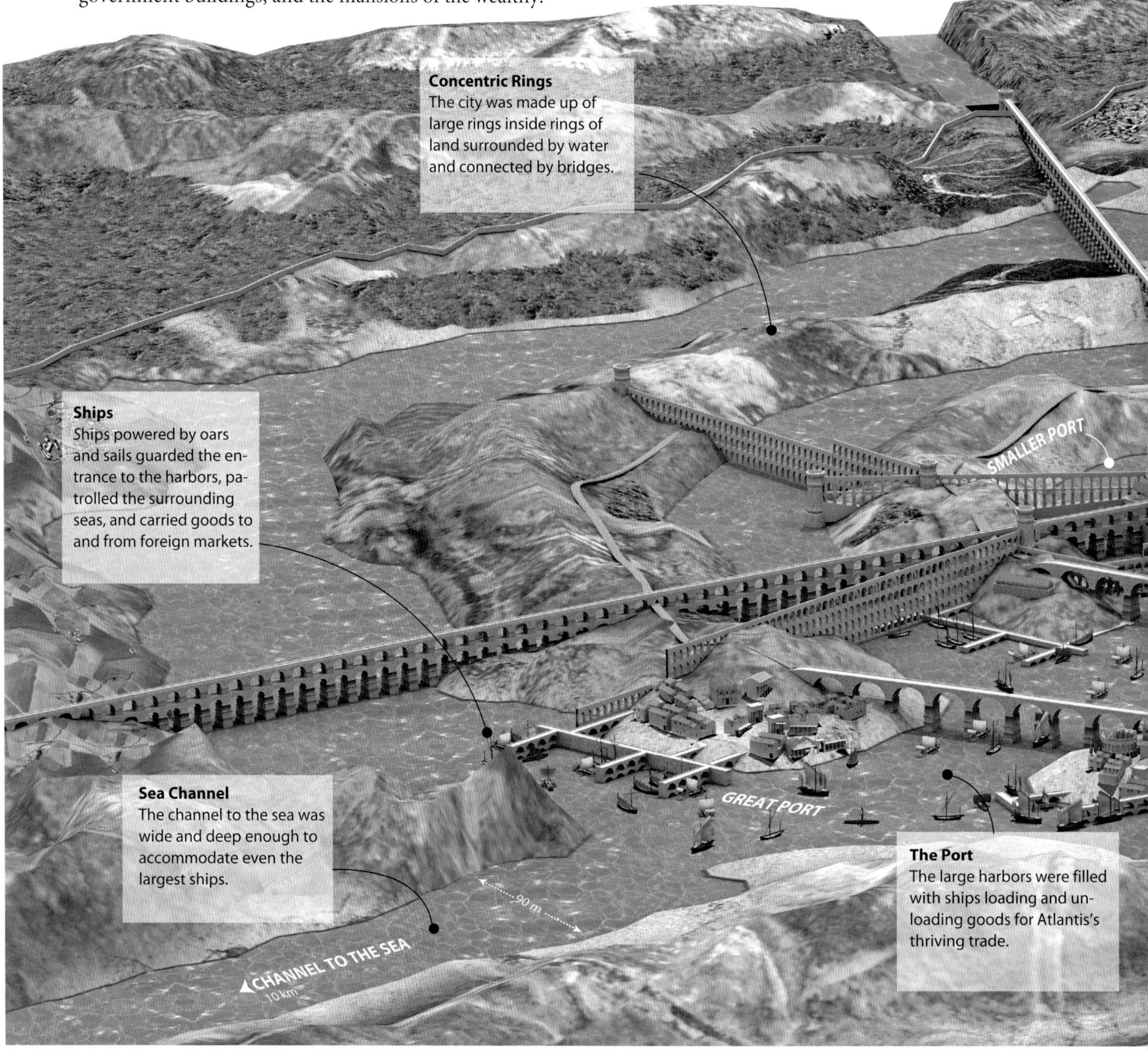

**Concentric Rings**
The city was made up of large rings inside rings of land surrounded by water and connected by bridges.

**Ships**
Ships powered by oars and sails guarded the entrance to the harbors, patrolled the surrounding seas, and carried goods to and from foreign markets.

**Sea Channel**
The channel to the sea was wide and deep enough to accommodate even the largest ships.

**The Port**
The large harbors were filled with ships loading and unloading goods for Atlantis's thriving trade.

SMALLER PORT

GREAT PORT

90 m

CHANNEL TO THE SEA
10 km

# How many people lived in Atlantis?

Plato wrote that Atlantis had a much larger population than Athens. During the time of the war between Atlantis and Athens, Athens had some 20,000 warriors plus many more nonfighting citizens and slaves. Some later accounts of the doomed island have estimated the population at from 6 million to 10 million people.

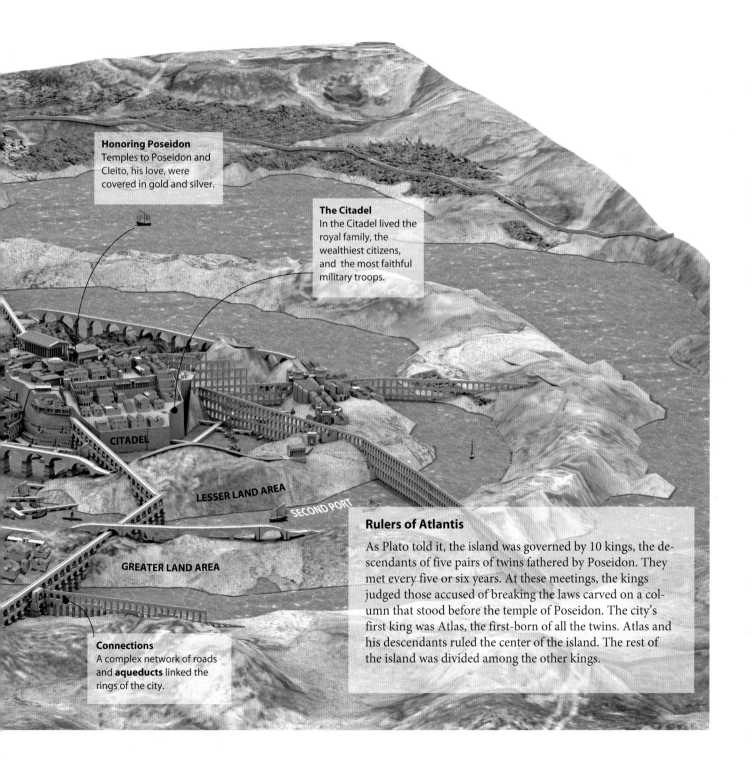

**Honoring Poseidon**
Temples to Poseidon and Cleito, his love, were covered in gold and silver.

**The Citadel**
In the Citadel lived the royal family, the wealthiest citizens, and the most faithful military troops.

CITADEL

LESSER LAND AREA

SECOND PORT

GREATER LAND AREA

**Connections**
A complex network of roads and **aqueducts** linked the rings of the city.

## Rulers of Atlantis

As Plato told it, the island was governed by 10 kings, the descendants of five pairs of twins fathered by Poseidon. They met every five or six years. At these meetings, the kings judged those accused of breaking the laws carved on a column that stood before the temple of Poseidon. The city's first king was Atlas, the first-born of all the twins. Atlas and his descendants ruled the center of the island. The rest of the island was divided among the other kings.

# Life in Atlantis

Atlantis, which was established with the help of the Greek gods, was perfect until the people became corrupt.

At the time Poseidon became the lord of Atlantis, the island consisted of only a low mountain and a fertile plain. To create a city for himself and his love Cleito, he used his divine powers to circle the mountain with two rings of land and three rings of water. The god also created two magnificent streams—one hot and one cold—to carry water from the sea to the land.

Poseidon supplied the island with everything his children and their descendants would need. A mild climate, rich soil, and an irrigation network ensured bountiful harvests. Fruit trees filled the air with rich fragrances. In the island's many forests and pastures lived many kinds of animals, including herds of elephants. Mines yielded copper, silver, gold, and **orichalcum**—a legendary metal second only to gold in value.

## BUILDING A CITY

The Atlanteans used their excellent engineering skills to construct a magnificent city. From abundant deposits of rock, they quarried material to build harbors and docks. The busy harbor was filled with sturdy and roomy cargo ships with one square sail. On the docks was piled the bounty of the island, awaiting export to the people of nearby islands and coastal towns.

Tall bridges spanned the rings of water to connect the rings of land. Three protective walls of artistically arranged white, black, and red stone ringed the island. The outermost wall was covered with brass. The middle wall was covered with tin.

The third wall surrounded the center of the island, where the Atlanteans built a mighty **citadel.** The wall around the Citadel was covered with *orichalcum* (a legendary metal) so that it glowed red in the sunlight.

In the Citadel were temples and a sacred grove dedicated to Poseidon. The grove was rich in beautiful flowers and tall trees. Outside the temple were golden statues of the rulers and their wives.

## MAGNIFICENT CITY

The wealth of the kingdom was also displayed in its elegant buildings and the magnificent mansions inhabited by the ruling classes. All homes, even those of ordinary citizens, had hot and cold running water.

Spread throughout the city were parks and temples. Like the Greeks, the Atlanteans adorned their parks and open areas with monuments and sculptures, particularly of **Nereids** (sea nymphs) riding dolphins. Atlantis also had many fountains. A track for athletic competitions circled the island.

The Atlanteans also built many ponds and pools both outdoors and indoors. In winter, the indoor pools served as public baths. To prevent flooding, **aqueducts** carried the water to the sea.

Atlantis displayed its wealth not only in its architecture, but also its libraries and public teaching areas. There, the wisdom of the older members of society was honored.

## The Citadel

Inside the Citadel were two temples. The first, which was dedicated to Poseidon and Cleito, was enclosed by a wall made of gold. The second temple, dedicated only to Poseidon, was covered with silver and gold. The roof was made of ivory and decorated with gold, silver, and the highly prized metal orichalcum. Orichalcum also covered the inner walls of the temple.

Dominating the temple was a statue of Poseidon so huge that its head touched the roof. The god stood in a chariot pulled by six winged horses. Surrounding him were 100 *Nereids* riding dolphins.

Outside the temple, the Atlanteans had erected golden statues of all the descendants of the 10 original kings as well as their wives. There was also an altar where the kings offered **sacrifices** to the god. Around the temples were the royal palace and the mansions of the wealthy.

## Jules Verne (1828-1905)

was a French visionary who wrote some of the first science-fiction stories. He foresaw the invention of airplanes, television, guided missiles, and space satellites. He even accurately predicted how they would be used. Verne's stories are fantastic tales of adventure that are supported by cleverly used realistic detail and believable explanations. They carry readers over, under, and above Earth. *Twenty Thousand Leagues Under the Sea,* published in 1870, follows Captain Nemo, who cruises the oceans in a submarine.

In Verne's *Around the World in Eighty Days* (1873), Phileas Fogg travels around Earth in the then-unheard-of time of 80 days, just to win a bet. Other Verne thrillers include *A Journey to the Center of the Earth* (1864), *From the Earth to the Moon* (1865), and *Around the Moon* (1870).

Verne's first novel, *Five Weeks in a Balloon* (1863), brought him immediate success. It was based on an essay he wrote describing the exploration of Africa in a balloon. The essay was rejected several times before one publisher suggested that Verne rewrite it as a novel of imagination.

# Rediscovering Atlantis

In *20,000 Leagues Under the Sea,* French novelist Jules Verne includes a fantastic journey to the submerged ruins of Atlantis by the mad Captain Nemo and the professor who tells the tale.

We arrived at a preliminary plateau where ... *picturesque* [interesting] ruins took shape, betraying the hand of man, not our Creator. They were huge stacks of stones in which you could distinguish the indistinct forms of palaces and temples, now arrayed in hosts of blossoming *zoophytes* [such animals as corals and sea anemones], and over it all, not ivy but a heavy mantle of algae and *fucus plants* [a type of brown algae].

But what part of the globe could this be, this land swallowed by cataclysms? Who had set up these rocks and stones like the *dolmens* [burial mounds] of prehistoric times? Where ... had Captain Nemo's fancies taken me?

I wanted to ask him. ... I seized his arm. But he shook his head, pointed to the mountain's topmost peak. ... I followed him with one last burst of energy and ... scaled the peak, which crowned the whole rocky mass by some ten meters [30 feet].

I looked back down the side we had just cleared. .... My eyes scanned the distance and took in a vast area lit by intense flashes of light. In essence, this mountain was a volcano. Fifty feet below its peak, amid a shower of stone and slag, a wide crater vomited torrents of **lava** that were dispersed in fiery cascades into the heart of the liquid mass. So situated, this volcano was an immense torch that lit up the lower plains all the way to the horizon.

In fact, there beneath my eyes was a town in ruins, demolished, overwhelmed, laid low, its roofs caved in, its temples pulled down, its arches dislocated, its columns stretching over the earth ... farther off, the remains of a gigantic **aqueduct;** here, the caked heights of an acropolis along with the fluid forms of a *Parthenon* [temple]; there, the remnants of a *wharf* [boat dock], as if some bygone port had long ago harbored merchant vessels and triple-tiered war galleys on the shores of some lost ocean; still farther off, long rows of collapsing walls, deserted thoroughfares, a whole Pompeii buried under the waters. ... Where was I? Where was I? I had to find out at all cost. ...

But Captain Nemo came over and stopped me with a gesture. Then, picking up a piece of chalky stone, he advanced to a black basaltic rock and scrawled this one word:

**ATLANTIS**

What a light shot through my mind. ... Atlantis of Plato ... I had it there now before my eyes ... The region thus engulfed was beyond Europe, Asia, and Lybia, beyond the columns of Hercules where those powerful people the Atlantides lived, against whom the first wars of ancient Greece were waged.

Thus led by the strangest destiny, I was treading under foot the mountains of this continent, touching with my hand those ruins a thousand generations old and contemporary with the geological *epochs* [periods of time]. I was walking on the very spot where the contemporaries of the first man had walked.

My heavy soles were crushing the skeletons of animals from the age of fable, animals that used to take cover in the shade of these trees now turned to stone!

# Where Was Atlantis?

Over the centuries, scholars, explorers, and **archaeologists** have proposed many locations for the lost island. The three most commonly suggested sites are the **Iberian** Peninsula, the Atlantic Ocean, and the Mediterranean or Aegean seas.

**SUPPORT FOR THE IBERIAN HYPOTHESIS**

**1** **1592**
Priest Juan de Maria was the first to link the Atlantis of Plato with Spain.

**2** **1673**
José Pellicer de Ossau Salas y Tovar linked Spain to Atlantis. He maintained that the island with the Temple of Cleito was located at the mouth of the Guadalquivir.

**3** **1801**
Writer Fabre d'Olivet stated that Atlantis was found in the Western Mediterranean, between Spain and Morocco.

**4** **1803**
Naturalist Jean Baptiste Bory de Saint-Vincent hypothesized that the Canary Islands off the coast of Spain are part of the island that disappeared.

**5** **1874**
Geographer and archaeologist E. F. Berlioux identified the mythical island with the Atlas Mountains in Morocco and Gibraltar.

**6** **1911**
Juan Fernández Amador de los Ríos proposed that Atlantis was Tartessos and the Iberian Peninsula.

**7** **1920**
Geologist Aimé-Louis Rutot maintained that Atlantis was in Morocco.

**8** **1922**
Archaeologist Adolf Schülten considered Atlantis to be Andalusia (a region in southern Spain) and the kingdom of the Tartessians.

**9** **1928**
Elena Wishaw, director of the Ancient Mediterranean Research Association, placed the underwater remnants of the capital of Atlantis off the coasts of Cadiz.

**10** **1984**
*Philologist* (scientist who studies languages) Jorge María Ribero-Meneses pointed out connections between Tartessians, Tartars, and the Titans and proposed that the Egyptians and Phoenicians came from Cantabria (northern Spain).

**11** **1994**
Georgeos Díaz-Montexano maintained that the center of Atlantis was the south of Spain (Tartessos) and Morocco.

**12** **2001**
Jacques Collina-Girard believed that Atlantis could be found at the mouth of the Strait of Gibraltar, on the island of Spartel.

Yucatán Coast (Mexico)

Atlantic Ocean

Bimini Islands (Bahamas)

Lake Titicaca (Bolivia)

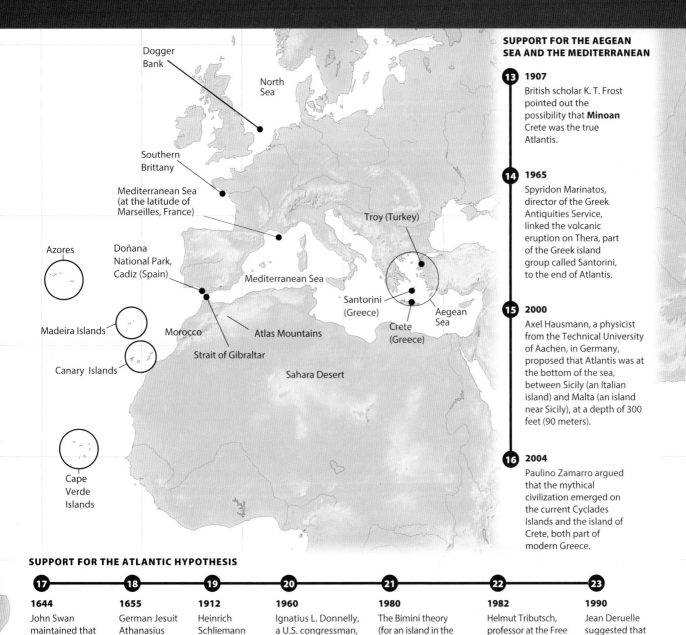

Dogger Bank

North Sea

Southern Brittany

Mediterranean Sea (at the latitude of Marseilles, France)

Azores

Doñana National Park, Cadiz (Spain)

Madeira Islands

Morocco

Canary Islands

Strait of Gibraltar

Cape Verde Islands

Mediterranean Sea

Atlas Mountains

Sahara Desert

Troy (Turkey)

Santorini (Greece)

Crete (Greece)

Aegean Sea

## SUPPORT FOR THE AEGEAN SEA AND THE MEDITERRANEAN

**13** **1907**
British scholar K. T. Frost pointed out the possibility that **Minoan** Crete was the true Atlantis.

**14** **1965**
Spyridon Marinatos, director of the Greek Antiquities Service, linked the volcanic eruption on Thera, part of the Greek island group called Santorini, to the end of Atlantis.

**15** **2000**
Axel Hausmann, a physicist from the Technical University of Aachen, in Germany, proposed that Atlantis was at the bottom of the sea, between Sicily (an Italian island) and Malta (an island near Sicily), at a depth of 300 feet (90 meters).

**16** **2004**
Paulino Zamarro argued that the mythical civilization emerged on the current Cyclades Islands and the island of Crete, both part of modern Greece.

## SUPPORT FOR THE ATLANTIC HYPOTHESIS

**17** **1644**
John Swan maintained that Atlantis was found in the Atlantic.

**18** **1655**
German Jesuit Athanasius Kircher stated that Atlantis was between Europe and America.

**19** **1912**
Heinrich Schliemann placed Atlantis close to the Azores Islands and Madeira, both now part of modern Portugal.

**20** **1960**
Ignatius L. Donnelly, a U.S. congressman, placed Atlantis on the Azores Islands.

**21** **1980**
The Bimini theory (for an island in the Bahamas, located in the Caribbean Sea) was developed by several writers: J. Manson Valentine, Charles Berlitz, and Pierre Carnac.

**22** **1982**
Helmut Tributsch, professor at the Free University of Berlin, proposed the isle of Gavrinis, near Carnac in Brittany (an area in the northwest of France).

**23** **1990**
Jean Deruelle suggested that Atlantis was in the North Sea on Dogger Bank.

**THE ROCK OF GIBRALTAR,**
which dominates the British
overseas territory of Gibraltar, is
the northern pillar of the **Pillars
of Hercules.**

# The Pillars of Hercules

Since ancient times, the passage that connects the Mediterranean Sea with the Atlantic Ocean has been identified with one of the greatest heroes of Greek **myths.**

**THE STRAIT OF GIBRALTAR** connects the Mediterranean Sea and the Atlantic Ocean. It also separates Europe and Africa.

In his story of Atlantis, Plato places the lost island beyond the Pillars of Hercules. Since ancient times, people have understood that this name refers to two huge rocks on either side of what is now known as the Strait of Gibraltar. This narrow body of water connects the Mediterranean Sea and the Atlantic Ocean.

The Strait of Gibraltar also separates Europe and Africa. There, only 8 to 23 miles (13 to 37 kilometers) of water lie between Morocco and the southernmost part of Spain and the British overseas territory of Gibraltar.

The rock on the northern (European) side of the strait is the Rock of Gibraltar. This huge limestone mass—1,398 feet (426 meters) at its highest point—takes up most of Gibraltar's 2 1/2 square miles (6.5 square kilometers).

The identity of the southern (African) rock is less clear. Both Jebel Musa and Monte Hacho in Morocco have been identified as the other pillar.

## INTO THE UNKNOWN

For thousands of years, the peoples living around the Mediterranean Sea thought the Pillars of Hercules marked the end of the known world. According to one story, the words *Non plus ultra,* meaning *Nothing farther beyond,* were carved on the pillars as a warning to those foolhardy enough to try to sail through the passageway.

## WHY HERCULES?

The rocks at the Strait of Gibraltar were named for Hercules because of his quest to steal a prized herd of cattle. According to Greek **myth,** Hercules was the son of Zeus, the king of the gods, and the princess Alcmene (alk MEE nee). Hera, the wife of Zeus, was jealous of Alcmene and hated Hercules. Hera caused Hercules to have a fit of madness, during which he killed his wife, Megara, and their children.

The **oracle** at Delphi told Hercules that he had to serve King Eurystheus of Tiryns for 12 years to purify himself of the murders. Eurystheus commanded Hercules to perform 12 labors.

For the 10th labor, Eurystheus ordered Hercules to journey to an island at the far western edge of the world. There he was to capture the famous red cattle of Geryon, a giant with three heads, six legs, and six arms.

In some accounts, Hercules created the rocky pillars by breaking through a mountain that blocked his way. In other accounts, he set up the pillars to honor the memory of his journey.

**A STATUE OF HERCULES** grasping two massive pillars overlooks the port city of Ceruta, Spain, on the southern side of the Strait of Gibraltar.

# Atlantis and the Thera Volcano

Tales about the devastation on the Aegean islands of Thera and Crete may have provided the inspiration for Plato's story of Atlantis.

The legend of Atlantis may have begun with a massive volcanic eruption on a tiny island in the Aegean Sea in about 1600 B.C. At that time, the island, called Thera, was the home of an artistic and prosperous people who had adopted many customs from the **Minoans.** The Minoan **culture,** which arose on the nearby island of Crete, was the first important civilization in Europe.

The eruption in 1600 B.C. was not the first major blast from the Thera volcano, but it was one of its largest. In fact, it was one of the largest eruptions in the past 10,000 years.

A column of gas and **volcanic ash** shot some 20 miles (32 kilometers) into the sky. When the column collapsed, Thera and a surrounding area at least the size of Arizona—including Crete—were plunged into total darkness. Searing clouds of ash and gas raced over Thera. Geological excavations on the island have uncovered ash deposits more than 165 feet (50 meters) thick.

## A SUDDEN COLLAPSE

The eruption also spewed out at least 7.2 cubic miles (30 cubic kilometers) of **magma,** about the same volume as that of all the ice covering Antarctica. The loss of such a huge amount of magma caused the roof of the **magma chamber** to collapse.

Much of Thera disappeared, suddenly transformed into a huge depression called a *caldera* that quickly filled with water. Today, the western and southern shorelines of Thera and the eastern shoreline of neighboring Therasia mark the edge of this caldera. It is 7$\frac{1}{2}$ miles (12 kilometers) wide and some 1,300 feet (400 meters) deep.

Many scientists believe the eruption also triggered **tsunamis.** The waves, which would have been massive when they reached Crete, destroyed all in their path.

## DESTRUCTION OF CRETE

Some scholars believe that the eruption and its effects dealt a death blow to Crete and the Minoan civilization. If so, tales of the *cataclysm* (great flood, earthquake, or other sudden change to the Earth) must surely have been passed down over generations by other Mediterranean peoples. Perhaps an Egyptian version of the story some hundreds of years later inspired a Greek **philosopher** to create his story of a lost island.

## SANTORINI

The deep blue water of the Aegean Sea fills an ancient volcanic caldera at Santorini. The two largest islands in the group, Thera (left) and Therasia (far left), mark the lip of a caldera created in a massive eruption in 1600 B.C. The smaller islands between them formed in later eruptions of the volcano.

# Frozen in Time

Ash from the eruption of the Thera volcano buried the thriving seaport of Akrotiri on the western coast of Thera. Archaeological excavations have revealed houses with open courtyards, workrooms, and storerooms at ground level. Living quarters above had windows and decorated walls.

# Before the Eruption

Before the eruption of the volcano in about 1600 B.C., Thera was a major trading center of the **Minoan** civilization, which arose on Crete. Although typical of island towns of that time, Thera was apparently larger and contained massive and complicated architecture. Perhaps thousands of farmers, fishers, traders, and craft workers lived there. The island was covered with trees and flowers, and blessed with streams and birds.

**AKROTIRI** wwas destroyed in the eruption of the Thera volcano in about 1600 B.C.

# The Glory of Thera

The excavations made at Thera, also known as Santorini, allow the reconstruction of an ancient society connected with the existence of Atlantis. Houses and several *amphorae* (AM fuh ree—tall, two-handled earthenware jars) were found under a coating of volcanic residues. There are also beautiful **frescoes** (wall paintings) of images of daily life.

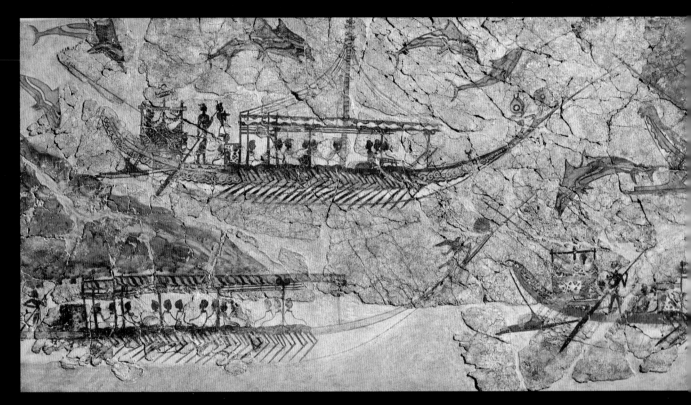

## The Flotilla Fresco

**Minoan** ships appear to sail between two island cities in one part of a fresco found wrapped around three walls of a room in the ruins of Akrotiri. The complete fresco is 39 feet (12 meters) long but only 17 inches (43 centimeters) high. Scholars have long debated the meaning of the fresco.

### DOLPHIN VASE

Artists on Thera frequently used images of animals, especially dolphins and other sea creatures, to decorate pottery, jewelry, and wall paintings.

**SACRED WAY**
Ancient ruins of a city on Thera line a path that once led to a shrine dedicated to the god Apollo.

**HONORING THE GODS**
A man, marked as a servant of the gods by his partially shaved head and nudity, holds fish that will become a **sacred** offering.

decorate the northern *portico* (covered porch) at the Palace of Knossos on Crete.

## Sir Arthur Evans

Much of what we know about the **Minoans** comes from excavations conducted on Crete in the early 1900's by Sir Arthur Evans, a British **archaeologist.** Evans's work confirmed his theory that the people of ancient Crete had created a **culture** different from that in Greece or any other area around the Aegean Sea.

Born in England in 1851, Evans was already a noted scholar when he first visited Crete in 1894. Long interested in the ancient history of the island, he visited the ancient settlement of Knossos *(kuh NOS uhs* or *NOS uhs)*, which he bought with his own money. He began excavating there in 1900.

Knossos, which was first settled in 7000 B.C., became the chief political and ceremonial center of the Minoan civilization. At Knossos, Evans uncovered a sprawling complex of buildings. He was convinced that the complex was the palace of King Minos. But later scholars have suggested that the palace might have been a *necropolis* (city of the dead) or a temple. At Knossos, Evans also found clay tablets bearing the earliest form of Greek writing.

Evans published his discoveries in a multivolume work called *Palace of Minos* (1922-1935). He was knighted in 1911 and died in 1941.

# A Story of Ancient Crete

Many scholars and writers have linked the downfall of Crete and the Minoan civilization that developed there to the destruction of Plato's Atlantis.

The people living on Crete when the Thera volcano erupted are known to us as the Minoans. Sir Arthur Evans, a British archaeologist, named the people of the islands after Minos, a legendary king of Crete.

The Minoans were one of four cultures that flourished on the islands and shores of the Aegean Sea between about 3000 and 1100 B.C. The other cultures included the Mycenaeans (MY suh NEE uhnz), who thrived on the mainland of Greece, and the western Anatolians, whose culture was centered in the city of Troy in modern-day Turkey.

The fourth culture was that of the Cycladic people, who flourished on Thera and a number of neighboring islands. By 1900 B.C., however, the Cycladic culture had declined and had adopted many features of the Minoan and Mycenaean cultures.

### MINOAN ART

The Minoans developed the first important European civilization. They made great advances in architecture, art, and engineering. They built beautiful palaces with spacious courtyards. The finest known Minoan architectural achievement was the Palace of Minos, constructed in about 1500 B.C. in the town of Knossos. This complex and sprawling structure had dozens of rooms built around a courtyard. Wooden columns supported the beams of the ceiling.

### EVANS AT KNOSSOS
Sir Arthur Evans (in the white suit) poses with excavation workers at the Palace of Knossos on Crete. Evans bought the site himself before beginning his digging there.

# Minos and the Minotaur

According to Greek **myth,** Minos (MY nuhs) was the king of Crete. He asked Poseidon to send him a bull from the sea as a sign of the god's favor. Minos promised to **sacrifice** the bull to Poseidon. But the bull was so beautiful that Minos refused to kill it. Angered, Poseidon caused Minos's wife, Pasiphae (puh SIHF uh ee), to fall in love with the bull.

In time, Pasiphae gave birth to the Minotaur (MIHN uh tawr), a monster that had the head of a bull but the body of a man. Minos ordered Daedalus (DEHD uh luhs), a skilled craftsman and inventor, to build the Labyrinth (LAB uh rihnth), a mazelike building, to imprison the Minotaur. The Labyrinth had so many dark tunnels and twists and turns that people who entered never found their way out.

Minos went on to conquer much of Greece, including Athens. As a display of his power, he forced the Athenians to send him seven young men and seven young women every year as a sacrifice to the Minotaur. After many young Athenians had been eaten by the Minotaur, Theseus (THEE see uhs), the son of the king of Athens, volunteered to go to Crete and kill the monster.

Theseus succeeded in his plan with the help of Minos's daughter Ariadne (AR ee AD nee), who had fallen in love with him. She gave him a sword and a magic ball of thread that Daedalus had given her. Theseus tied the end of the thread to the door of the Labyrinth then dropped the ball on the floor. The ball silently led him through the twisting tunnels straight to the Minotaur. Catching the Minotaur as he slept, Theseus cut off his head. Theseus and Ariadne then fled from Crete.

Minos imprisoned Daedalus for helping Theseus and Ariadne run away, but Daedalus escaped. Minos pursued Daedalus and finally found him in Sicily. According to one story, Daedalus killed the king by scalding him in a specially constructed bathtub.

**Minoan** builders divided these beams into three horizontal sections, called the *architrave* (AHR kuh trayv), the *frieze* (freez), and the *cornice* (KAWR nihs). The three sections together are called the *entablature* (ehn TAB luh chur). The entablature became a vital part of later Greek building.

The Minoans also built palaces in other towns. All Minoan palaces served as administrative and commercial centers as well as royal residences. The great age of Minoan architecture lasted from about 2000 to 1450 B.C.

The Minoans decorated the walls and floors of their buildings with spectacular paintings in bold colors. Minoan artists often depicted subjects from nature, including plants and animals of both the land and sea. Many paintings show religious processions and festivals, along with images of goddesses. The Minoans also excelled at making pottery and jewelry, which they traded profitably throughout the Aegean region and in Egypt. Minoan designs were widely copied.

### MINOAN ENGINEERING

The Palace of Knossos had a network of **terra-cotta** (baked clay) pipes that supplied drinking water. The water came mainly from cisterns on hilltops that collected rain water. The palace also had flushing toilets, through which water ran constantly. The waste flowed into sewers and was carried out to the sea. Air shafts above the drainage system served as vents.

### MINOAN WRITING

Clay tablets unearthed by Arthur Evans in Minoan ruins on Crete revealed that the Minoans had developed the earliest forms of writing ever found in Europe. Evans named the two unique but somewhat similar systems of writing Linear A and Linear B. The scripts soon became one of the great mysteries of **archaeology** as scholars repeatedly failed to decipher the writing.

Finally, in 1953, Michael Ventris, a British amateur *cryptographer* (code breaker), solved the puzzle of Linear B. Several years earlier, Alice Kober, an American classics professor, had determined that the complex symbols in Linear B represented syllables of words. Building on Kober's work, Ventris proved that Linear B had been used to write ancient Greek. The Mycenaeans on the Greek mainland later adapted the Minoan writing system to their language.

Linear A, however, is still a puzzle. Older than Linear B, Linear A seems to have been used to write an entirely different language. That language remains unknown today.

### THE DISAPPEARANCE OF THE MINOANS

Sometime after about 1450 B.C., fire destroyed nearly all the towns and palaces on Crete. Although the palace in Knossos was damaged, it survived, and Mycenaeans gained control of it. Minoan culture began to decline after the palace was lost. The Mycenaeans abandoned the palace in the early 1300's B.C. The culture disappeared in about 1100 B.C.

**BULL-LEAPING**
A young man flips over the back of a charging bull in the *Bull-Leaping Fresco* from the Palace of Knossos. Two women, distinguished by their much lighter skin, stand in front of and behind the bull. Scholars disagree whether the Minoans actually practiced this sport.

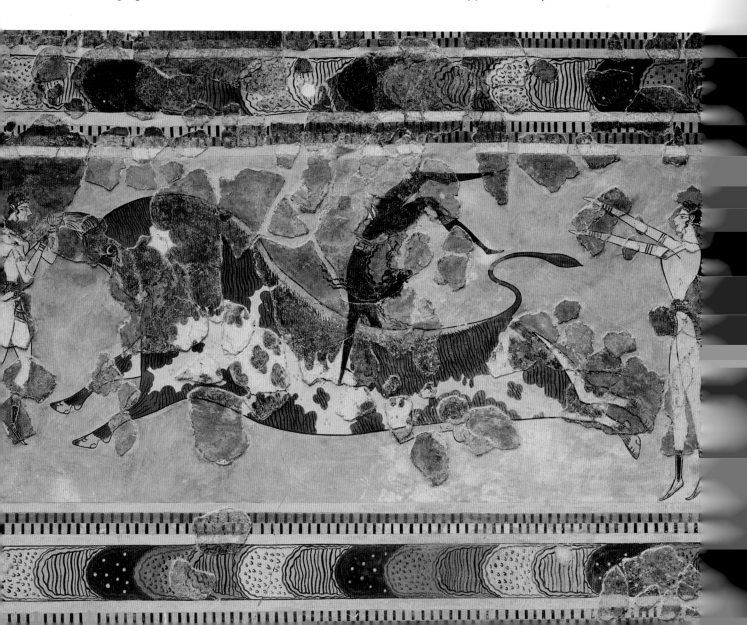

# The Remains of a Culture

The **Minoans** were skilled artists who created impressive sculptures, often in gold and other precious metals, and pottery decorated with beautiful images and patterns. Splendid **frescoes** in brilliant colors decorated the walls of their palaces and other buildings.

## The Bull in Minoan Art and Culture

The bull was a central element of Minoan **culture**. It symbolized masculine fertility. The bull appeared in frescoes, on pottery and jewelry, and as figurines. Bull horns marked Minoan religious sanctuaries, where bulls were **sacrificed** to the gods. Some scholars believe Minoans jumped over the backs of bulls during religious ceremonies or athletic competitions, as shown in frescoes.

According to Greek **myth,** King Minos of Crete kept a half-human, half-bull monster in a mazelike building called a Labyrinth. This monster, called the Minotaur, was the offspring of the king's wife and a bull. In the Cretan city of Knossos, archaeologists discovered a palace with many confusing passageways that may have been the site of the Cretan Labyrinth.

**MYSTERIOUS DISK**

A disk found at Phaistos, an archaeological site on Crete, dates from about 1700 B.C. It is covered with symbols, arranged in a spiral pattern, that scholars have not been able to read.

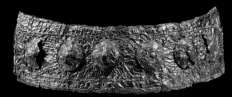

**GOLDSMITHING**

The Minoans enjoyed wearing necklaces, pendants, and bracelets made of gold. The names of the owners are inscribed on some of the pieces.

## MINOAN DRESS

Delicate necklaces and bracelets adorn three women with elaborately styled hair in a **fresco** called *Ladies in Blue* from the Palace of Knossos. The women, who likely represent members of the court, are dressed in closely fitted dresses that narrow dramatically at the waist. A fresco called *The Prince of the Lilies* may represent a priest. Archaeologist Arthur Evans added the man's skirt to the painting.

## VESSELS

Vessels made of fired clay were widely used by the Minoans. The vessels' shapes were related to their intended use, from collecting and holding water and oil to storing seeds and grains.

## ELEGANT POTTERY

The vase shown above, at left, depicting *Labryses* (double-headed axes), associated with the worship of goddesses, which were among the most common symbols used on Minoan vessels. The Minoans also favored patterns from nature.

## SNAKE GODDESS

A ceramic statue of a woman holding two snakes, found at Knossos, may represent a goddess or priestess. The statue which is 13.5 inches (34.3 centimeters) tall, dates to about 1600 B.C. Many similar statues have been found in Knossos.

# Destruction from the Sea

Scientific evidence suggests that gigantic waves triggered by the eruption of the Thera volcano could have devastated Crete.

By the early 1900's, scientists knew that Thera had been devastated by a massive volcanic eruption. Some scientists theorized that the eruption might also have caused the fall of the **Minoan** civilization on nearby Crete. But was the explosion the complete story?

## WATER FROM A VOLCANO

In the mid-1900's, some scientists suggested that a **tsunami** might have played a major role in the Minoans' downfall. A tsunami is a series of large ocean waves. Tsunamis can be produced by an earthquake or a landslide. They may also result from the eruption of a volcano in or under the ocean. The eruption pushes a huge column of ocean water upward. This "hump" of water quickly ripples outward.

As the waves enter shallow water along a coastline, they slow and grow. The 1883 eruption of Krakatau, a volcano in Indonesia, produced waves up to 130 feet (40 meters) high. The eruption of Thera in 1600 B.C. was even more powerful.

## TSUNAMI EVIDENCE

Excavations on Crete have uncovered strong evidence that a powerful tsunami could have struck the island at the same time that the Thera volcano erupted. In deposits found far above sea level, scientists have unearthed beach pebbles, sea shells, and tiny ocean animals mixed with pottery and other Minoan objects. Only a tsunami could account for the presence of these natural objects, they concluded.

## TSUNAMI EFFECTS

The tsunami would have severely damaged or even destroyed Crete's seaports and coastal towns. Merchant and navy ships would have been smashed. Many people would have drowned.

Cropland, timberlands, and streams disappeared under layers of **volcanic** ash 40 to 120 feet (12 to 36 meters) thick. Ash lofted high into the atmosphere may have even blocked enough sunlight to lower temperatures in the region for months. Farming would have become difficult.

**Archaeological** evidence shows that in about 1450 B.C., fire destroyed nearly all the towns and palaces on Crete. Clay tablets found on the island show that the Minoan civilization did not die out immediately. But if a tsunami also struck about that time, it likely swept away much of the Minoans' power. With a crippled economy and a weakened population, the Minoans became easy prey for the Mycenaeans, who overran the island some 50 years later.

# Atlantis in the Atlantic

Plato placed Atlantis "beyond the **Pillars of Hercules.**" For hundreds of years, people have searched the Atlantic Ocean for the lost island.

The eastern Atlantic Ocean, beyond the Pillars of Hercules, has long been a focus in the search for Atlantis. In the *Middle Ages* (from around the 400's to the 1400's A.D. in Europe), one scholar proposed that the Canary Islands and the neighboring islands of Madeira and the Azores were all that survived of the lost island. The conquest of the Americas led the Spaniards to a new hypothesis: The Antilles were another remnant of the lost continent. Centuries later, in *Twenty Thousand Leagues Under the Sea* (1870), French author Jules Verne imagined that the islands of Madeira, the Azores, the Canaries, and Cape Verde were once the highest peaks on Atlantis.

### ATLANTIS AND THE CONGRESSMAN

One of the earliest and most enthusiastic advocates for an eastern Atlantic location for the lost island was Ignatius Donnelly. Once a member of the United States Congress from Minnesota, Donnelly aroused great popular interest in Atlantis with his best-selling book *Atlantis: The Antediluvian World* (1882).

In the book, he claimed that Plato's Atlantis was an actual island that lay within a triangle formed by Madeira, the Azores, and the Canaries. On Atlantis, Donnelly said, early human beings developed the first civilization, then spread throughout the world to establish new cultures and civilizations. He argued that supposed similarities between the **cultures** of ancient Egypt and Central America proved that these cultures had shared a common origin.

But, according to Donnelly, Atlantis met its doom when a comet zoomed close by Earth. As Earth passed through the comet's tail, fire, stones, and gravel rained down, destroying the island and causing it to sink into the sea. Donnelly's theories became so popular that expeditions were launched to search for the remnants of Atlantis in the Americas, northwest Africa, and the **Iberian** Peninsula.

### ATLANTIS AND GEOLOGY

Since Donnelly published his theories, scientists have explored the floor of the Atlantic Ocean using ships, research submarines, Earth-orbiting satellites, and computers. They have found huge plains that spread across the seafloor and long mountain chains that rise toward the surface of the water. They have charted volcanoes that erupt from the ocean bottom and deep trenches and valleys. But scientists generally agree that no geologically convincing evidence for the existence of a large sunken island has ever been found.

# Underwater Exploration

Many efforts to locate the lost island of Atlantis have involved *marine* (ocean) **archaeology.** Scientists search for and study archaeological evidence underwater by diving and by using devices that can gather information about an object without actually touching it.

## Exploring the Deep

Marine archaeologists engage in two kinds of diving. In ambient diving, the diver's body is exposed to the pressure of the *ambient* (surrounding) water. Archaeologists also explore the ocean in vehicles that protect them from the dangerous effects of water pressure.

## Underwater Detection

Marine archaeologists use a variety of technologies to search underwater for such evidence of ancient cultures as pottery and other objects, ships, or the remains of buildings. These devices function as extensions of the human senses.

**SONAR**
A method called sonar scanning helps detect underwater objects by the reflection of sound waves.

**SENSORS**
These electronic devices measure temperature and movement and identify chemical elements.

## Alvin

The submersible *Alvin,* launched in 1964 by the Woods Hole Oceanographic Institution in Massachusetts, can dive to a depth of 14,750 feet (4,500 meters). Its steel pressure hull was designed to carry a pilot and two scientists on dives lasting from 6 to 10 hours.

# Underwater vehicles

## DIVING

Sophisticated equipment allows underwater archaeologists to stay underwater longer and go deeper than they could by holding their breath. Divers can wear a tank that holds compressed air or a special mixture of breathing gases. They can also get air or breathing gas through a hose connected to air pumps on a boat.

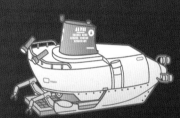

## SUBMERSIBLES

Piloted submersibles have extremely strong hulls and can descend to about 21,000 feet (6,500 meters), farther than submarines.

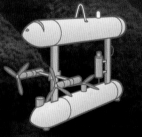

## ROV

Small, remotely-operated underwater vehicles (ROV's) are used to reach places that are too small, deep, or dangerous for divers to go. These robotic devices are equipped with lamps and video cameras. Some ROV's also have sensors for recording water conditions and mechanical arms for grasping objects.

## AUV

The most advanced robots are completely autonomous, meaning they can move without people directing them. These Autonomous Underwater Vehicles (AUV) are guided by computer programs and sensors of all types.

## MAGNETOMETER

This device measures magnetic fields given off by rocks, metal, and buried objects.

## CAMERAS

Photographs of objects or photographic maps of sites can be made from submarines or by divers carrying underwater cameras.

## ROBOTIC ARM

Some vehicles are equipped with robotic arms for moving objects and sediments.

## TRANSPONDERS

These electronic devices can receive a radar or other signal and automatically transmit a response.

# Places to See and Visit

## OTHER PLACES OF INTEREST

### THE GIBRALTAR MUSEUM
#### GIBRALTAR

The island of Gibraltar, which lies off the southern coast of Spain, forms one side of the Strait of Gibraltar, which connects the Mediterranean Sea and Atlantic Ocean. Rocks at the eastern end of the strait are known as the **Pillars of Hercules,** beyond which Plato located Atlantis. The rich past of Gibraltar can be seen in the museum's vast **archaeological** records.

### BIMINI MUSEUM
#### ALICE TOWN, THE BAHAMAS

Some people have argued that North, South, and East Bimini once belonged to the road system of the lost city of Atlantis. The museum, located in the city of Alice Town on the North Island, is dedicated to the preservation of the history and **culture** of the people of the islands. It has a valuable collection of utensils and other objects, some of which were discovered in nearby coral reefs. Praised for its documents, photos, and varied *artifacts* (human-made objects), the museum is one of the biggest attractions on the islands.

### BRITISH MUSEUM
#### LONDON

The British Museum is one of the oldest and most famous museums of ancient artifacts in the world. Objects from Crete include discoveries from the palace of Knossos as well as ancient pottery, bronze statues, and stone vases found elsewhere on Crete.

## Yonaguni Monument

An enormous stone formation discovered off the Japanese island of Yonaguni in 1986 (right) represents the remains of a lost city, according to one theory. The formation, which is said to include such human-made features as columns and walls, supposedly sank into the ocean during an earthquake from 2,000 to 3,000 years ago. Most scientists who have explored the formation, however, believe the rocks were shaped by such natural processes as earthquakes and erosion.

## The Bimini Road

This odd underwater rock formation nearly 0.6 miles (1 kilometer) in length is located to the north of Bimini Island, in the Bahamas. The formation is natural, but many see in it the structure of a road or wall, the remains of a lost city.

### NATIONAL ARCHAEOLOGICAL MUSEUM OF ATHENS

GREECE

The museum contains the richest existing collection of objects from ancient Greece, from sculptures to urns and small objects. The museum's library has a valuable collection of records of archaeological excavations and is the most significant archive of publications on Greek archaeology.

### THERA PREHISTORIC MUSEUM

SANTORINI, GREECE

The museum displays a collection of **frescoes** and objects discovered at the archaeological site of ancient Akrotiri, during excavations supported by the Archaeological Society of Athens. The museum also has objects found during excavations at a nearby archaeological site named Potamos. Parts of the collection—vases, cups and jugs—are delicately painted with familiar *motifs* (themes), which can also be found on the murals of the city, from women dressed in Minoan dresses to scenes of the city.

# Glossary

**Aqueduct**—An artificial channel through which water is moved to the place where it is used.

**Archaeologist**—A scientist who studies the remains of past human cultures.

**Bull-leaping**—A sport, supposedly practiced by the Minoans, in which a person flips over the back of a bull.

**Caldera**—A large depression that forms when the ground above a magma chamber collapses.

**Citadel**—The center of the legendary island of Atlantis, which contained temples, a grove dedicated to Poseidon, a royal palace, and mansions of the wealthy.

**Culture**—A term used by social scientists for a way of life. Culture includes a society's arts, beliefs, customs, institutions, inventions, language, technology, and values. A culture produces similar behavior and thought among most people in a particular society.

**Dialogue**—A literary form that consists of a conversation between two or more people.

**Fresco**—A painting made on damp plaster, using pigments mixed with water.

**Hellenes**—Ancient Greek-speaking people.

**Iberia**—The peninsula occupied today by the countries of Spain and Portugal.

**Lava**—Magma that flows onto Earth's surface.

**Magma**—Molten rock below the ground.

**Magma chamber**—A region beneath a volcano where magma builds up.

**Minoans**—One of four cultures that flourished on the islands and shores of the Aegean Sea between about 3000 and 1100 B.C.

**Myth**—Stories told to explain the world and its mysteries.

**Nereid**—A sea nymph.

**Oracle**—An ancient shrine where people came to seek advice from people who were believed to have the power to reveal the will of the gods and to foretell the future. The word also refers to the prophet and prophetess at the shrine, and to their prophecy.

**Orichalcum**—A legendary metal mined in Atlantis that was second only to gold in value.

**Philosopher**—A scholar who studies such topics as knowledge, good, and *existence* (being).

**Pillars of Hercules**—Huge rocks that mark the boundary between the Mediterranean Sea and the Atlantic Ocean; in ancient times, they marked the end of the known world.

**Plague**—A deadly outbreak of disease.

**Ritual**—A solemn or important act or ceremony, often religious is nature.

**Sacrifice**—Something killed and offered up to a god.

**Sacred**—A thing that is holy or worshipped.

**Terra-cotta**—A kind of baked clay that is hard and durable.

**Tsunami**—A series of large, destructive waves.

**Tyrant**—A dictator.

**Virtue**—Moral excellence that is acquired by consciously developing particular qualities of character or by consciously following high moral principles. One who has virtue is called virtuous.

**Volcanic ash**—Fine material thrown out of a volcano during an eruption.

# For Further Information

## Books

Abrams, Dennis. *Atlantis*. New York: Chelsea House, 2012. Print.

Howe, John. *Lost Worlds*. New York: Kingfisher, 2009. Print.

Walker, Kathryn, and Brian Innes. *The Mystery of Atlantis*. New York: Crabtree Pub., 2010. Print.

Webb, Stuart. *Atlantis and Other Lost Worlds*. New York: Rosen Pub., 2013. Print.

Woyt, Barbara A., and Ann Lewis. *Searching for Atlantis*. New York: Rosen Central, 2012. Print.

## Websites

"Atlantis." *History.com*. A&E Television Networks, 2014. Web. 03 Mar. 2014.

Bowers, Andy. "We've Found The Lost City Of Atlantis ... Again." *NPR*. NPR, 18 Nov. 2004. Web. 03 Mar. 2014.

Drye, Willie. "Atlantis-True Story or Cautionary Tale?" *National Geographic*. National Geographic Society, 2014. Web. 02 Mar. 2014.

Hefner, Alan G. "Atlantis: The Myth." *Encyclopedia Mythica*. Encyclopedia Mythica, 2004. Web. 05 Mar. 2014.

Stewart, Iain. "Echoes of Plato's Atlantis." *BBC History*. BBC, 17 Feb. 2011. Web. 03 Mar. 2014.

# Index

# Acknowledgments

Pictures:

© Alamy Images

© G. Dagli Orti, De Agostini Picture Library/Bridgeman Art Library

© Werner Forman Archive/Bridgeman Art Library

© Jacques Collina Girard

© Corbis Images

© Getty Images

NASA

© National Geographic Stock

© Science Source

© Shutterstock

© Virgin

© Woods Hole Oceanographic Institution